Tracking
the Blue Beast

Written by Becca Heddle

Illustrated by Liliana Perez

Collins

On Tuesday night, I hear loud sounds.

The next day, we go to play at Elroy's flat.
My sister spots tracks on the ground.

"Let's scout for clues," I say.
We look around the tower blocks.

I have found blue fur.
Elroy ties some to his belt.

Footprints in the dirt lead us to
the railway tracks.

The birds have stopped chirping.

The beast must be near.

Elroy spies a cloud of blue steam from the playground.

The beast is as still as a statue. The blue steam leaks from its mouth.

"Do you think it might eat boys?"
says Elroy.

The beast's seat is a mound of tins.

I think it eats beans.

Beast spotters zoom around the corner.

"Look out!" cries Elroy.
Dust swirls around a flash
of blue.

A shout comes from the avenue.
"It must not get away!"

The tins shift to reveal gleaming blue snouts in a swirl of fur. Little beasts!

We must outwit the spotters, so that the beast comes back.

"We can trick them," I say.

Beast sounds spout from the speaker.
The spotters get their snaps and retreat.

The beast has come back.

It feeds beans to its little ones.

The next day ... The beasts zoom away into the skies.

"Come back one day!" we shout.
I'm so proud we rescued them.

Tracking the beast